HODOPILE TOURS

SWEDEN TRAVEL GUIDE

Contents

SWEDEN TRAVEL GUIDE:

E xplore the Natural Beauty and Cultural Treasures of Sweden

WELCOME TO SWEDEN!

This stunning country offers some of the world's most spectacular scenery, from snow-capped mountains and lakes to lush forests and stunning coastline. Whether you're looking for a relaxing vacation, an adventurous holiday, or anything in between, Sweden has something for everyone. From its vibrant cities to its picturesque countryside, Sweden is an ideal destination for any traveler. In this travel guide, you'll find all the information you need to plan and enjoy your trip, including top attractions, activities, dining, and accommodation. So, let's get started exploring the best of Sweden!

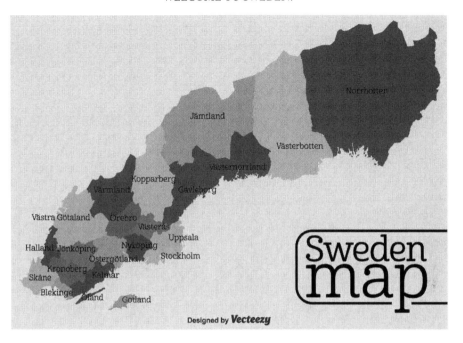

INTRODUCTION TO SWEDEN

A. Geography

Sweden is a Nordic country located in Northern Europe, on the Scandinavian Peninsula. With an area of 447,435 square kilometers, Sweden is the fifth-largest country in Europe and the largest in Northern Europe. It has a population of 10.2 million people, making it the most populous of the Nordic countries.

Sweden is bordered by Norway to the west, Finland to the northeast, and the Baltic Sea to the east, with the Kattegat and Skagerrak straits connecting it to Denmark in the south. Sweden is divided into three distinct geographical regions: Norrland in the north, Svealand in the central region, and Götaland in the south.

Norrland is the largest region in Sweden, covering almost 60% of the total area. It is a sparsely populated area with vast forests, deep lakes, and mountain ranges. The highest mountain in Sweden, Kebnekaise, is located in Norrland.

Svealand is the second-largest region in Sweden, encompassing the provinces of Uppland, Södermanland, and Västmanland. This region is mostly characterized by its vast plains and rolling hills. The capital city of Stockholm is located in Svealand, on the eastern coast of the country.

Götaland is the third and smallest region in Sweden. It is comprised of the provinces of stergötland, Smland, Halland, Västergötland, and Bohuslän. This region is known for its many lakes, forests, and valleys, as well as its coastline along the Kattegat and Skagerrak straits. The cities of Gothenburg and Malmö are located in Götaland.

Sweden has a varied geography, with some of the most beautiful landscapes in Europe. From the rugged mountains and glaciers of Norrland to the coastal towns and rolling hills of Götaland, Sweden has something to offer every traveler. Whether you're looking to explore the wilderness, take in the sights of the cities, or just relax in the countryside, Sweden is sure to provide an unforgettable experience.

B. History

Sweden has a long and storied history that dates back to prehistoric times. Evidence of human habitation in Sweden dates back to at least 11,000 BCE. During the Stone Age, inhabitants of Sweden built megalithic tombs, rock carvings, and petroglyphs.

The Viking Age is a significant chapter in Swedish history. During this period, the Vikings were a powerful force in Europe, spreading their influence and culture through trade, raiding, and colonization. The Vikings were known for their shipbuilding skills, and they established settlements in the Baltic region, Scandinavia, the British Isles, and parts of the Mediterranean.

In the early Middle Ages, Sweden was divided into a number of small kingdoms. By the 12th century, Sweden had become a unified kingdom and a Christian nation. Sweden went on to become a major power in Europe, and during the 16th century, it was one of the most powerful countries in the world. During this period, Sweden fought numerous wars with its neighbors, including Denmark, Norway, and Poland.

In the 18th century, Sweden underwent a period of significant political change. The country abolished its absolute monarchy and adopted a more liberal form of government, known as the Age of Liberty. This period saw the development of a strong sense of national identity, and Sweden emerged as an independent nation in the 19th century.

During the 20th century, Sweden underwent a period of rapid economic growth and modernization. Today, Sweden is one of the most prosperous countries in the world and has a high standard of living. It is known for its progressive social policies, environmental sustainability, and commitment to human rights.

Sweden has a rich cultural heritage, and it is home to a wealth of historical sites and monuments. From ancient Viking settlements to medieval castles, churches, and royal palaces, there is something for every type of traveler. Tourists can also explore the country's stunning natural beauty, from its beautiful coastline to its pristine forests and majestic mountains. With its vibrant cities, vibrant culture, and fascinating history, Sweden is a must-visit destination for any traveler.

C. Culture

Sweden is a country of beautiful landscapes, vibrant culture, and a rich history.

Sweden is known for its focus on sustainability and is a leader in environmental protection. The Swedes also value innovation, and the country is known for its advanced technology and industrial development. This is evidenced by the many Swedish companies that have made a major impact on the world, such as Volvo and IKEA.

The culture of Sweden is strongly influenced by its Nordic roots, and the country is known for its strong sense of community, equality, and freedom. Swedes are known to be very welcoming and open to people of all backgrounds, and they place a high value on personal integrity and respect for others.

Swedish culture is also heavily shaped by its traditional music and dance. Traditional Swedish folk music is a way to express emotion, and it is often accompanied by singing and dancing as well as traditional instruments such as the fiddle and accordion.

Sweden is also known for its unique cuisine. The country is known for its fresh, local ingredients, and dishes such as herring, gravlax, and Swedish meatballs are popular throughout the country. Swedish cuisine also has influences from other countries, including Finland and Germany.

Sweden is a beautiful country with a lot to offer visitors, and the culture and history of Sweden makes it an ideal destination for any traveler. The country is known for its natural beauty, its vibrant culture, and its impressive advancements in technology and sustainability. Whether you are looking for a relaxing holiday or a thrilling adventure, Sweden is sure to have something for you.

PLANNING YOUR TRIP

A. When to Visit

S weden is a beautiful and diverse country that has something to offer to all kinds of travelers. From the vibrant cities of Stockholm and Gothenburg to the stunning natural landscapes of Lapland, Sweden is a country rich in culture, history, and breathtaking scenery.

If you're looking for the best time to visit Sweden, it really depends on what kind of experience you're hoping to have.

Summer in Sweden is the most popular time to visit, and for good reason. The days are long, with around 18 hours of daylight in the peak of June and July, and temperatures can reach a balmy 25 degrees. Summer is the ideal time to explore the archipelagos in the south of the country, as well as marvel at the spectacular Northern Lights in Lapland.

Autumn is also a great time to visit Sweden, as the changing colors of the leaves provide a picturesque backdrop to the cities. The days are still relatively long, and temperatures are pleasant and mild. Autumn is the perfect time of year to explore the national parks and forests, as well as get to know the culture and history of Sweden.

Winter in Sweden is a magical time of year, with snow-covered landscapes and the occasional sighting of the Northern Lights. During this time of year, many ski resorts are open, as well as unique Christmas markets and festive activities. While it is colder, temperatures rarely drop below -10 degrees

Celsius.

Springtime in Sweden is a great time to visit for those who want to avoid the crowds. Temperatures are mild and the days are longer, making it the perfect time to explore the outdoors.

No matter what time of year you visit Sweden, you're sure to have an unforgettable experience. From stunning natural landscapes to vibrant cities, Sweden is a country full of beauty and culture.

1. **Where to Stay**

Sweden is a popular tourist destination for visitors from around the world. With its stunning natural beauty, vibrant cities, and unique culture, Sweden has something to offer everyone.

If you're looking for a luxurious vacation, then the capital city of Stockholm is the ideal destination. Here, you'll find a range of luxurious hotels, with the Grand Hôtel being the most famous. Located in the heart of the city, this iconic hotel offers stunning views of the Royal Palace and Gamla Stan, the old town. Other luxurious options include the Radisson Blu Strand Hotel, located on the waterfront in Stockholm, and the Scandic Anglais, a modern hotel with a rooftop terrace and views of the city.

If you're looking for a more budget-friendly option, then Gothenburg is the perfect destination. Here, you'll find a range of mid-range and budget hotels, including the Clarion Hotel Post and the Comfort Hotel Göteborg. Both of these hotels offer comfortable and modern rooms, as well as convenient access to the city's attractions.

For a unique experience, consider staying in one of the many small towns and villages scattered across Sweden. Many of these towns have a range of traditional accommodation options, including bed and breakfasts, guesthouses, and hostels. Some of the most popular destinations include the idyllic village of Ystad, the charming coastal town of Visby, and the beautiful mountain village of Åre.

Finally, if you're looking for an unforgettable experience, then consider spending a few nights in one of Sweden's many national parks. Here, you can find a range of comfortable accommodation options, from cabins and cottages to campsites. Popular national parks include Abisko National Park, Sarek National Park, and Stora Sjöfallet National Park, all of which offer breathtaking views and unique wildlife experiences.

i. Hotels in Stockholm

Stockholm is one of the most beautiful cities in Europe and it is also a great destination for travelers. There is no shortage of hotels in Stockholm, so tourists can choose from a variety of accommodations. From luxurious 5 star resorts to cozy budget-friendly hostels, there is something for everyone in Stockholm. Here is a guide to some of the best hotels in Stockholm for tourists.

Luxury Hotels in Stockholm

1. Grand Hôtel Stockholm – Located on the waterfront, Grand Hôtel Stockholm is a 5-star hotel with a Michelin-starred restaurant, a spa, and a bar. It offers modern, stylish rooms and a range of amenities such as a fitness center, sauna, and a terrace. Prices is at about €250 per night.

2. Scandic Anglais – Located in the heart of Stockholm, Scandic Anglais is a 4-star hotel with a modern Scandinavian design. It offers luxurious rooms with all the necessary amenities, a restaurant, a bar, and a fitness center. Prices start at €180 per night.

3. Hotel Skeppsholmen – Located on an island in Stockholm's harbor, Hotel Skeppsholmen is a 4-star hotel with an elegant, classic design. It offers modern rooms with all the necessary amenities, a restaurant, a bar, and a spa. Prices start at €200 per night.

4. Lydmar Hotel – Located in the city center, Lydmar Hotel is a 5-star hotel with a contemporary design. It offers luxurious rooms with all the necessary amenities, a restaurant, a bar, and a fitness center. Prices start at €220 per night.

5. Haymarket by Scandic – Located in the city center, Haymarket by Scandic is a 4-star hotel with a modern design. It offers luxurious rooms with all the necessary amenities, a restaurant, a bar, and a fitness center. Prices start at €150 per night.

6. Hotel Diplomat – Located in the city center, Hotel Diplomat is a 5-star hotel with a modern, luxurious design. It offers stylish rooms with all the necessary amenities, a Michelin-starred restaurant, a bar, and a spa. Prices start at €260 per night.

7. Radisson Blu Waterfront Hotel – Located on the waterfront, Radisson Blu Waterfront Hotel is a 4-star hotel with a modern design. It offers luxurious rooms with all the necessary amenities, a restaurant, a bar, and a spa. Prices start at €170 per night.

8. Hotel Rival – Located in the city center, Hotel Rival is a 4-star hotel with a modern, stylish design. It offers luxurious rooms with all the necessary amenities, a restaurant, a bar, and a fitness center. Prices start at €160 per night.

9. Nordic Light Hotel – Located in the city center, Nordic Light Hotel is a 4-star hotel with a modern, Scandinavian design. It offers luxurious rooms with all the necessary amenities, a restaurant, a bar, and a fitness center. Prices start at €180 per night.

10. Hotel At Six – Located in the city center, Hotel At Six is a 5-star hotel with a modern, luxurious design. It offers stylish rooms with all the necessary amenities, a restaurant, a bar, and a spa. Prices start at €220 per night.

Budget Friendly Hotels in Stockholm

1. City Backpackers Hostel – Located in the city center, City Backpackers Hostel is a 3-star hostel with a modern design. It offers basic rooms with all the necessary amenities, a restaurant, a bar, and a fitness center. Prices start at €60 per night.

2. Hotel Birger Jarl – Located in the city center, Hotel Birger Jarl is a 3-star hotel with a modern, Scandinavian design. It offers basic rooms with all the necessary amenities, a restaurant, a bar, and a fitness center. Prices start at €80 per night.

3. Hotel Hornsgatan – Located in the city center, Hotel Hornsgatan is a 3-star hotel with a modern design. It offers basic rooms with all the necessary amenities, a restaurant, a bar, and a fitness center. Prices start at €90 per night.

4. City Hotel Oden – Located in the city center, City Hotel Oden is a 3-star hotel with a modern, Scandinavian design. It offers basic rooms with all the necessary amenities, a restaurant, a bar, and a fitness center. Prices start at €60 per night.

5. STF Stockholm Hostel – Located in the city center, STF Stockholm Hostel is a 3-star hostel with a modern design. It offers basic rooms with all the necessary amenities, a restaurant, a bar, and a fitness center. Prices start at €50 per night.

6. STF Långholmen Hostel – Located on an island in Stockholm's harbor, STF Långholmen Hostel is a 3-star hostel with a modern design. It offers basic rooms with all the necessary amenities, a restaurant, a bar, and a fitness center. Prices start at €50 per night.

7. Generator Stockholm – Located in the city center, Generator Stockholm

is a 3-star hostel with a modern design. It offers basic rooms with all the necessary amenities, a restaurant, a bar, and a fitness center. Prices start at €60 per night.

8. STF Södermalm Hostel – Located on Södermalm, STF Södermalm Hostel is a 3-star hostel with a modern design. It offers basic rooms with all the necessary amenities, a restaurant, a bar, and a fitness center. Prices start at €50 per night.

9. First Hotel Reisen – Located in the city center, First Hotel Reisen is a 3-star hotel with a modern, Scandinavian design. It offers basic rooms with all the necessary amenities, a restaurant, a bar, and a fitness center. Prices start at €70 per night.

1. Hotel C Stockholm – Located in the city center, Hotel C Stockholm is a 3-star hotel with a modern, Scandinavian design. It offers basic rooms with all the necessary amenities, a restaurant, a bar, and a fitness center. Prices start at €80 per night.

ii. Camping in Sweden

Sweden is an ideal destination for campers, offering a wide variety of beautiful and serene locations to choose from. From the stunning Swedish alpine mountains to the lush forests and tranquil lakes, there is something for everyone.

Sweden is also home to some of the best camping spots in the world. With a variety of options from luxury camping resorts to rustic wilderness campsites, Sweden has something for everyone.

The best places to go camping in Sweden depend on the type of experience you are looking for. For those looking for a luxury camping experience, there are a number of resorts that offer fully equipped cabins and lodges with all the comforts of home. Some of the best luxury camping resorts in Sweden include Tännforsen Resort and Norrland Resort in Åre, and SkiStar Sweden Resort in Åre.

For those looking for a more rustic camping experience, there are plenty of wilderness camping sites throughout Sweden. These campsites offer a tranquil, natural setting and often come with basic amenities such as fire pits, picnic tables, and toilets. The best wilderness camping sites in Sweden include Kebnekaise, Stora Sjöfallet, and Sarek National Parks.

No matter where you decide to camp in Sweden, you can expect to pay anywhere from $10-30 per night for a campsite. Some of the luxury camping resorts may cost more, but they often include additional amenities such as hot tubs, saunas, and on-site restaurants.

Sweden is a country of beauty and adventure, making it the perfect destination for campers. Whether you're looking for a luxury camping resort or a rustic wilderness campsite, you're sure to find the perfect spot in Sweden. So pack your bags, grab your tent, and get ready to explore the great outdoors!

C. Getting Around

Traveling around Sweden can be an exciting experience, especially with the help of a travel guide. There are several options available for tourists to get around in Sweden, such as trains, buses, and car rentals. Each of these transportation options vary in price and convenience, so it is important to consider the best option for your travel plans.

Train

Sweden has an extensive and efficient railway system that connects all major cities. Trains are typically the fastest and most convenient way to get around. Travelers can purchase tickets online or at the station, and prices vary depending on your destination and travel class. For example, a ticket from Stockholm to Gothenburg costs around 200 SEK for second-class seating and 250 SEK for first-class seating.

Bus

Buses are another popular transportation option for travelers in Sweden. Most cities in Sweden have regular bus service, and prices are typically cheaper than train tickets. For example, a ticket from Stockholm to Gothenburg costs around 100 SEK. Buses are slower than trains and often make multiple stops, so travelers should plan accordingly.

Car Rental

Car rental is also an option for travelers in Sweden. Car rental prices vary depending on the type of car, duration of rental, and insurance options. The minimum age to rent a car in Sweden is 18 and a valid driver's license is required.

Trams

Trams are also available in the larger cities in Sweden, and they are typically the quickest way to get around. A single-journey ticket will cost around 30 SEK (roughly 3 USD).

Taxis

Taxis are available in most cities in Sweden, and they are a convenient way to get around. Prices will vary depending on the distance travelled, but a short trip will typically cost around 60 SEK (roughly 6 USD).

Overall, getting around in Sweden is quite easy for tourists. Public transportation is reliable, affordable, and convenient, while rental cars and taxis are also available. With a little bit of research, tourists can easily find the best way to get around Sweden.

SIGHTS AND ATTRACTIONS

Natural Wonders

Sweden is a country full of natural wonders that are sure to leave any visitor with lifelong memories. From the vast forests and archipelagos of the north, to the rolling hills and stunning lakes of the south, Sweden has something to offer everyone.

1. Stockholm archipelago: The Stockholm archipelago is a stunning collection of more than 24,000 islands and islets, located in the Baltic Sea. With vast forests, glistening lakes, secluded beaches and quaint fishing villages, it's the perfect place to explore Sweden's unique and varied nature. You can take a boat trip to explore the islands and admire the views, go kayaking, or simply enjoy a picnic on the beach.

2. High Coast: The High Coast is a beautiful stretch of coastline in the north of Sweden, featuring stunning cliffs, white sandy beaches, and crystal clear waters. This national park is home to a variety of wildlife and is an ideal place for a nature lover. You can take a hike along the coast, or explore the picturesque villages and take in the breathtaking views of the sea.

3. Gotland: Gotland is a stunning island located off the east coast of Sweden. It is home to some of the most spectacular scenery in the country, with lush green forests, rugged coastline, and pristine beaches. You can explore the island's many medieval churches and ruins, or take a boat trip to visit the small islands and islets dotted around the coast.

4. Laponia: Laponia is a vast region located in the far north of Sweden, covering an area of almost 9,000 square kilometres. It is home to some of the most beautiful landscapes in the country, with vast forests, majestic mountains, and crystal clear lakes. You can explore the area on a wildlife safari, take a boat trip to admire the stunning views, or simply take a hike through the wilderness.

5. Åre: Åre is a popular ski resort in the Swedish mountains, located in the north of the country. This is the perfect place for winter sports lovers, with its well-groomed slopes and stunning views of the surrounding landscape. You can also take part in a variety of other activities, such as snowshoeing, kayaking, and mountain biking.

6. Visingsö: Visingsö is a beautiful island located in the middle of Lake Vättern. It is home to some of the most stunning scenery in the country, with lush forests, ancient ruins, and crystal clear waters. You can explore the island on foot, take a boat trip around the lake, or simply relax on the peaceful beaches and admire the views.

7. Gårdsjö: Gårdsjö is a picturesque village located in the heart of Sweden. It is home to some of the most beautiful forests in the country, with ancient trees, rolling hills, and tranquil lakes. You can explore the village on foot, take a boat ride around the lake, or simply relax and admire the stunning views.

8. Höga Kusten: Höga Kusten is a breathtaking stretch of coastline located in the north of Sweden. It is home to some of the most stunning scenery in the country, with sweeping valleys, rugged cliffs, and white sandy beaches. You can take a boat trip to explore the area, go kayaking or swimming in the crystal clear waters, or simply relax and admire the views.

9. Kiruna: Kiruna is a small town located in the far north of Sweden, near the border with Norway. It is home to some of the most beautiful scenery in the country, with vast forests, stunning mountains, and crystal clear lakes.

You can explore the area on a snowmobile safari, take a boat trip on the river, or simply take a hike through the wilderness and enjoy the views.

10. Abisko National Park: Abisko National Park is a stunning area located in the far north of Sweden, near the border with Norway. It is home to some of the most beautiful landscapes in the country, with lush forests, rolling hills, and crystal clear lakes. You can take a cable car to the top of the mountain, take a boat trip on the lake, or simply take a hike and admire the views.

B. Cities and Towns

Sweden is a beautiful and diverse country with an abundance of natural beauty, rich culture, and vibrant cities and towns. From the vibrant capital city of Stockholm to the charming small towns of the Swedish countryside, there is something to explore in every corner of the country. Whether you want to experience the unique culture of the Sami people in the far north or explore the stunning archipelago in the south, Sweden has plenty of cities and towns to explore.

Cities

1. Stockholm: This vibrant city is the capital of Sweden and is home to stunning architecture, impressive museums, and a vibrant nightlife. Explore the old town of Gamla Stan, take a boat tour on the canals, and visit the Vasa Museum. Stockholm is also known for its many parks, gardens, and green spaces, as well as its stunning views of the Baltic Sea.

2. Gothenburg: Located on the west coast of Sweden, Gothenburg is a vibrant city full of culture and history. Explore the old town, take a boat tour to the

archipelago and visit the many museums. This city also has a lively music and nightlife scene, as well as some of the best seafood in the country.

3. Malmö: This city is located in the southern portion of Sweden, close to the Danish border. Malmö is known for its multicultural atmosphere and wide range of attractions, including art galleries, parks, and a popular beach. Spend some time in the old city center, explore the many museums and galleries, and visit the beautiful park of Pildammsparken.

4. Uppsala: Located about an hour north of Stockholm, Uppsala is one of the oldest cities in Sweden. Its main attraction is the Uppsala Cathedral, which was built in the 13th century. Visit the old university, explore the many parks and gardens, and take a boat tour on the Fyrisån River.

5. Lund: Located close to Malmö, Lund is a charming university city with a rich history and plenty of attractions. Explore the old town, visit the many museums and galleries, and take a boat tour to the island of Ven.

6. Linköping: Located in the heart of Sweden, Linköping is a vibrant city known for its historic old town and impressive cathedral. Explore the old town, visit the many museums and galleries, and take a boat tour on the Motala River.

7. Örebro: Located in the heart of Sweden, Örebro is a vibrant city known for its rich history, culture, and architecture. Explore the old town, take a boat tour on the Svartån River, and visit the many museums and galleries.

8. Helsingborg: Located on the south coast of Sweden, Helsingborg is a vibrant city with a rich history and plenty of attractions. Explore the old town, take a boat tour on the Öresund Strait, and visit the many museums and galleries.

9. Västerås: Located in the heart of Sweden, Västerås is a vibrant city known

for its impressive architecture, culture, and attractions. Explore the old town, visit the many museums and galleries, and take a boat tour on the Skena River.

10. Karlstad: Located in the heart of Sweden, Karlstad is a vibrant city known for its stunning architecture, culture, and attractions. Explore the old town, visit the many museums and galleries, and take a boat tour on the Klarälven River.

11. Borås: Located in the heart of Sweden, Borås is a vibrant city known for its unique architecture, culture, and attractions. Explore the old town, visit the many museums and galleries, and take a boat tour on the Viskan River.

12. Luleå: Located in the north of Sweden, Luleå is a vibrant city known for its stunning architecture, culture, and attractions. Explore the old town, take a boat tour on the Lule River, and visit the many museums and galleries.

13. Jönköping: Located in the heart of Sweden, Jönköping is a vibrant city known for its impressive architecture, culture, and attractions. Explore the old town, visit the many museums and galleries, and take a boat tour on the Vättern Lake.

14. Östersund: Located in the north of Sweden, Östersund is a vibrant city known for its unique culture, attractions, and stunning landscapes. Explore the old town, take a boat tour on the Österdalälven River, and visit the many museums and galleries.

15. Umeå: Located in the north of Sweden, Umeå is a vibrant city known for its impressive architecture, culture, and attractions. Explore the old town, visit the many museums and galleries, and take a boat tour on the Ume River.

16. Sundsvall: Located in the north of Sweden, Sundsvall is a vibrant city known for its unique culture, attractions, and stunning landscapes. Explore the old town, take a boat tour on the Indalsälven River, and visit the many

museums and galleries.

17. Gävle: Located in the heart of Sweden, Gävle is a vibrant city known for its impressive architecture, culture, and attractions. Explore the old town, take a boat tour on the Dalälven River, and visit the many museums and galleries.

18. Lidingö: Located in the east of Stockholm, Lidingö is an affluent island known for its green spaces, architecture, and attractions. Explore the old town, take a boat tour on the Mälaren Lake, and visit the many museums and galleries.

19. Norrköping: Located in the east of Sweden, Norrköping is a vibrant city known for its impressive architecture, culture, and attractions. Explore the old town, take a boat tour on the Motala Ström River, and visit the many museums and galleries.

20. Södertälje: Located in the south of Stockholm, Södertälje is a vibrant city known for its unique architecture, culture, and attractions. Explore the old town, take a boat tour on the Södertälje Canal, and visit the many museums and galleries.

Towns

1. Visby: Located on the island of Gotland, Visby is a charming medieval town with a rich history and plenty of attractions. Explore the old town, visit the many museums and galleries, and take a boat tour to the archipelago.

2. Marstrand: Located on the west coast of Sweden, Marstrand is a charming fishing village with a rich history and plenty of attractions. Explore the old town, take a boat tour on the Bohuslän Coast, and visit the many museums and galleries.

3. Ystad: Located on the south coast of Sweden, Ystad is a charming fishing

village with a rich history and plenty of attractions. Explore the old town, take a boat tour on the Öresund Strait, and visit the many museums and galleries.

4. Åre: Located in the north of Sweden, Åre is a charming ski resort with a rich history and plenty of attractions. Explore the old town, take a ski tour on the Åreskutan Mountain, and visit the many museums and galleries.

5. Höör: Located in the south of Sweden, Höör is a charming village with a rich history and plenty of attractions. Explore the old town, take a boat tour on the Mörrumsån River, and visit the many museums and galleries.

6. Falun: Located in the heart of Sweden, Falun is a charming mining town with a rich history and plenty of attractions. Explore the old town, take a mine tour on the Great Copper Mountain, and visit the many museums and galleries.

7. Älvdalen: Located in the north of Sweden, Älvdalen is a charming village with a rich history and plenty of attractions. Explore the old town, take a boat tour on the Älvdalen River, and visit the many museums and galleries.

8. Torsby: Located in the north of Sweden, Torsby is a charming village with a rich history and plenty of attractions. Explore the old town, take a boat tour on the Värmlandsån River, and visit the many museums and galleries.

9. Östhammar: Located in the east of Sweden, Östhammar is a charming fishing village with a rich history and plenty of attractions. Explore the old town, take a boat tour on the Åland Sea, and visit the many museums and galleries.

10. Malung: Located in the north of Sweden, Malung is a charming village with a rich history and plenty of attractions. Explore the old town, take a boat tour on the Dal River, and visit the many museums and galleries.

C. Cultural Attractions

Sweden is a country filled with cultural attractions and activities. From its stunning castles and palaces, to its vibrant music and art scenes, there is something for everyone in Sweden. With its rich history and culture, Sweden has something to offer both the casual tourist and the seasoned traveler.

For those interested in the country's history and culture, Stockholm is the best place to start. Stockholm is home to some of the most impressive castles and palaces in the world. For example, the Royal Palace and Drottningholm Palace are two of the most popular tourist attractions in Sweden. Both of these magnificent buildings offer visitors a glimpse into the past, and are sure to be a highlight of any trip.

In addition to the magnificent castles, Stockholm is home to several other cultural attractions. The Vasa Museum is a must-see for visitors, as it houses the well-preserved remains of a 17th century warship. Other popular sites include the City Hall, Skansen open-air museum, and the Fotografiska Museet.

Outside of Stockholm, there are many other cultural attractions. Gothenburg is Sweden's second largest city and is home to several interesting museums and galleries. The city also has a vibrant theater and music scene, and is well-known for its annual Gothenburg Culture Festival.

The Swedish countryside is also full of cultural attractions. Uppsala is home to the famous Uppsala Castle, as well as the Uppsala Cathedral. Other popular sites in the countryside include the Gripsholm Castle and the Göta Canal.

No matter what type of cultural attractions you're looking for, Sweden has something to offer. From its stunning castles and palaces, to its vibrant music and art scenes, there is something for everyone in Sweden. So if you're looking for a unique and memorable vacation, Sweden is the perfect destination.

Sweden is a country with a rich cultural heritage, and as such, has its own unique language and greetings. Understanding and using Swedish language and greetings is an important part of visiting and enjoying this beautiful country.

When greeting people in Sweden, it is customary to shake hands and introduce yourself. Swedish people are very polite, so it is important to show respect when greeting them. You should also use the appropriate formal or informal greeting depending on the situation.

In formal situations such as business meetings, you should use the formal greeting "God dag" which means "good day." This is usually accompanied by a handshake. In more informal settings, "Hej" is the most common greeting. This is a less formal version of "God dag" and is usually accompanied by a smile and a nod.

When speaking Swedish, you should use proper grammar and pronunciation. Most Swedes speak English, so you can get away with using a few incorrect words. However, it is still important to try to learn the basics of the language before you visit.

Common words and phrases you should learn include:

Hello – Hej
   Goodbye – Hej då
   Thank you – Tack
   Please – Snalla
   Yes – Ja
   No – Nej

Sweden has a rich cultural diversity, and you may encounter other languages and dialects during your visit. While Swedish is the official language, you may hear other languages such as Finnish, Sami, and Meänkieli. Respect these languages and greet people in Swedish to show that you appreciate the country's culture.

By understanding and using the proper language and greetings in Sweden, you can ensure that your visit is a pleasant and enjoyable one.

1. **ACTIVITIES AND EXPERIENCES**

A. Winter Activities

Sweden is a great destination for a winter holiday, with its spectacular landscape, beautiful cities, and great outdoor activities. Whether you're looking for a relaxing break or an adventure-filled holiday, Sweden has something for everyone.

Skiing and Snowboarding

Sweden is a great destination for skiing and snowboarding and has a variety
of resorts to choose from. Åre is one of the most popular and well-known ski

resorts in Sweden. Offering up to 18 lifts, a variety of slopes, and off-piste runs, it's the perfect place for ski and snowboard enthusiasts. Other resorts include Sälen, Vemdalen, and Årjäng.

Dog Sledding

Dog sledding is an exciting activity that is popular in Sweden's northern regions. You can either take a guided tour or rent your own team of huskies. There are plenty of companies offering dog sledding experiences, so you can choose one based on your preferences.

Ice Fishing

Ice fishing is a popular activity in Sweden and is a great way to experience the country's winter landscape. You can rent an ice fishing hut and fish for your own catch, or you can join a guided tour with a professional guide.

Snowmobiling

Snowmobiling is another great way to explore the Swedish winter landscape. You can rent a snowmobile and explore the countryside, or you can join a guided tour. Snowmobiling is a great activity for those who are looking for a more adventurous experience.

Northern Lights

The northern lights, also known as Aurora Borealis, is a breathtaking phenomenon that occurs in the night sky. Sweden is a great destination for viewing the northern lights, as it is located in the northern part of the country. Many tour companies offer special northern lights tours and activities, so you can make the most of your experience.

Ice Skating

Ice skating is a popular winter activity in Sweden and there are plenty of places to go skating. From lakes and ponds to indoor rinks, you can find plenty of places to go ice skating. You can also find ice skating trails in many parks, so you can explore the Swedish winter landscape while skating.

Cross-Country Skiing

Cross-country skiing is a great way to explore the Swedish countryside. You can rent your own equipment and explore the trails on your own, or you can join a guided tour. Cross-country skiing is a great way to get some exercise and explore the Swedish winter landscape.

Summer activities

Sweden is a beautiful country that offers a wide variety of activities for tourists to enjoy during the summer months. From outdoor adventures to cultural experiences, there's something for everyone in this stunning Scandinavian nation.

Outdoor Adventures

Sweden is an ideal destination for the outdoor enthusiast. From hiking and biking in the Swedish Alps to fishing in the crystal-clear lakes, there are activities for all skill levels. For those looking for an extreme adventure, there is white-water rafting, canyoning, and even heli-skiing. The breathtakingly beautiful Swedish countryside is perfect for a camping trip, and there are plenty of camping sites throughout the country.

Cultural Experiences

Sweden is a cultural hub, with a rich history and vibrant cities. Stockholm is a great place to explore the country's history and culture, with its cobblestone streets, historic buildings, and traditional cafes. Other cities like Gothenburg, Malmo, and Lund offer a variety of cultural activities, such as art galleries, museums, and theaters.

Relaxation

Sweden is also known for its stunning natural beauty, and there are plenty of opportunities to relax and rejuvenate. Take a stroll through the forest or take a dip in a secluded lake. Relax at a spa or take a boat ride along one of Sweden's many canals. For something a bit different, try a Viking sauna, a traditional Swedish experience.

Festivals and Events

Sweden is also known for its vibrant festivals and events. From traditional midsummer celebrations to music festivals, there's something for everyone. The Stockholm International Film Festival, held in the summer, is one of the biggest events in the country, and the Gothenburg International Film Festival is also worth a visit.

No matter what type of activity you're looking for, Sweden has something for everyone during the summer months. From outdoor adventures to cultural experiences, there's something for everyone in this beautiful Scandinavian nation.

1. Outdoor Activities

Sweden is a beautiful country with many outdoor activities to enjoy. From hiking and camping to skiing and kayaking, there is something for every type of outdoor enthusiast. Here are some of the best outdoor activities in Sweden for a tourist to enjoy:

1. Dog sledding: Dog sledding is an iconic activity in Sweden and an unforgettable way to explore the country's snowy landscape. For those looking for an adrenaline-pumping experience, dog sledding is a must-do activity.

2. Skiing and snowboarding: Skiing and snowboarding are two of the most popular outdoor activities in Sweden. With a variety of ski resorts, Sweden offers some of the best terrain in Europe.

3. Ice fishing: Ice fishing is a traditional Swedish activity that is still popular today. Ice fishing is a great way to explore the local culture and experience the beauty of the Swedish winter.

4. Snowshoeing: Snowshoeing is a great way to explore the Swedish wilderness. With a variety of trails, snowshoeing is a great way to get up close and personal with the nature of Sweden.

5. Hiking: Hiking is one of the most popular outdoor activities in Sweden. From coastal trails to mountain hikes, there is something for every type of hiker.

6. Volleyball: Volleyball is a popular beach activity in Sweden. With plenty of sandy beaches to choose from, there is no shortage of places to play.

7. Canoeing: Canoeing is a great way to explore the Swedish countryside. With a variety of lakes and rivers, there are plenty of opportunities to get out on the water.

8. Kayaking: Kayaking is a great way to explore the Swedish coast. With a

variety of kayaking routes, you can explore everything from fjords to small islands.

9. Mountain biking: Mountain biking is a great way to explore the Swedish countryside. With a variety of trails, there is something for every type of biker.

10. Sailing: Sailing is a popular activity in Sweden. With a variety of sailboats and yachts to choose from, you can explore the Swedish coastline in style.

11. Surfing: Surfing is a popular activity in Sweden. With a variety of beaches, there are plenty of places to catch some waves.

12. Windsurfing: Windsurfing is a great way to explore the Swedish coastline. With a variety of windsurfing spots, you can find the perfect conditions for your adventure.

13. Swimming: Swimming is a popular activity across Sweden. With a variety of lakes and rivers, there are plenty of places to take a dip.

14. Camping: Camping is a popular outdoor activity in Sweden. With a variety of camping spots, you can enjoy the beauty of the Swedish countryside.

15. Wildlife watching: Wildlife watching is a great way to explore the Swedish countryside. With a variety of animals and birds to watch, you can get up close to nature.

16. Horse riding: Horse riding is a popular activity in Sweden. With a variety of trails, you can explore the countryside in style.

17. Bird watching: Bird watching is a great way to explore the Swedish countryside. With a variety of birds to watch, you can get up close to nature.

18. Climbing: Climbing is a popular activity in Sweden. With a variety of climbing spots, you can explore the beauty of the Swedish landscape.

19. Geocaching: Geocaching is a great way to explore the Swedish country-side. With a variety of caches to find, you can explore the hidden gems of Sweden.

20. Snowmobiling: Snowmobiling is a popular activity in Sweden. With a variety of trails, you can explore the snowy landscape in style.

1. Food and Drink

Sweden is a great destination for food and drink enthusiasts. With its vast landscape and diverse cultural influences, Sweden is home to a wealth of culinary delights. From hearty Scandinavian classics to modern fusion dishes, Swedish cuisine offers something for everyone.

When it comes to drinks, Sweden is renowned for its craft beer, as well as its unique distilled spirits. Craft beer is especially popular, with microbreweries popping up all over the country. Sweden also has a thriving wine industry, with some excellent local varieties available.

When exploring the food scene in Sweden, it's important to sample the traditional dishes. Dishes like the classic Swedish meatballs, pickled herring, and smörgåsbord (a cold buffet of Scandinavian delights) are must-try dishes. Other popular dishes include pytt i panna (a hash made with potatoes and other vegetables) and gravad lax (cured salmon).

In terms of drinks, Swedish beer is among the best in the world. Popular brands include Carnegie Porter, Nils Oscar, and Haandbryggeriet. Swedish cider is also widely available, with the most popular brands being Rekorderlig and Kopparberg.

The Swedish distilled spirits scene is also worth exploring. Sweden is known for its aquavit, a spiced, herbal spirit. It can be enjoyed on its own or as part of a classic Swedish cocktail. Another popular spirit is brännvin, a grain-based spirit that is traditionally served with beer.

For those with a sweet tooth, Sweden has plenty of options. Prinsesstårta (princess cake) is a classic layered sponge cake with raspberry jam and whipped cream. And don't forget the local speciality Semla, a cardamom-flavoured sweet roll filled with almond paste.

From hearty traditional dishes to unique craft beverages, Sweden is a great destination for food and drink enthusiasts. Whether you're looking for a classic Swedish meal or an exotic fusion dish, Sweden has something to offer every palate.

i. Traditional Swedish Cuisine

For tourists visiting Sweden, exploring the country's traditional cuisine is an important part of experiencing the culture. Here's a look at some of the classic dishes and ingredients that make up traditional Swedish cuisine.

1. Köttbullar: Köttbullar, or Swedish meatballs, are a traditional Swedish dish. They are usually served with mashed potatoes, gravy, and lingonberries.

2. Räksmörgås: Räksmörgås is a popular Swedish dish that consists of a few slices of bread topped with shrimp and mayonnaise. It is usually served as a snack or light meal.

3. Pytt i Panna: Pytt i Panna is a traditional Swedish hash dish. It is made with diced potatoes, onions, and either beef, pork, or chicken. It is usually served with boiled eggs and pickled beets.

1. Janssons Frestelse: Janssons Frestelse is a traditional Swedish dish made with potatoes, anchovies, cream, and butter. It is typically served

throughout the holidays.

5. Gravad lax: Gravad lax is a popular Swedish dish of cured salmon. It is usually served with boiled potatoes, dill sauce, and mustard.

6. Falukorv: Falukorv is a popular Swedish sausage made with pork, beef, and spices. It is usually served with mashed potatoes and lingonberries.

7. Kalops: Kalops is a traditional Swedish stew made with beef, onions, potatoes, carrots, and spices. It is usually served with boiled potatoes, pickled beets, and lingonberries.

1. Toast Skagen: Toast Skagen is a popular Swedish dish made with toast, shrimp, mayonnaise, and dill. It is typically offered as an entrée.
2. 9. Herring: Herring is a popular Swedish dish made with pickled or marinated herring. It is usually served with boiled potatoes, chives, and sour cream.

10. Kåldolmar: Kåldolmar is a traditional Swedish dish of stuffed cabbage rolls. They are usually filled with beef, pork, rice, and spices and served with mashed potatoes and lingonberries.

11. Blodpudding: Blodpudding is a traditional Swedish dish of black pudding. It is usually served with mashed potatoes, lingonberries, and fried onions.

12. Kroppkakor: Kroppkakor are a traditional Swedish dish of potato dumplings stuffed with pork and spices. They are usually served with boiled potatoes and lingonberries.

13. Äggakaka: Äggakaka is a popular Swedish dish made with eggs, potatoes, onions, and bacon. It is usually served as a side dish or snack.

14. Raggmunk: Raggmunk is a traditional Swedish dish of potato pancakes. It is usually served with bacon, lingonberries, and fried onions.

15. Fiskbullar: Fiskbullar are a traditional Swedish dish of fish balls. They are usually served with mashed potatoes and lingonberries.

16. Prinskorv: Prinskorv is a popular Swedish sausage made with pork, beef, and spices. It is usually served with mashed potatoes and lingonberries.

17. Lutfisk: Lutfisk is a traditional Swedish dish of dried cod. It is usually served with boiled potatoes, bacon, and mustard sauce.

18. Köttsoppa: Köttsoppa is a traditional Swedish soup made with beef and vegetables. It is usually served with boiled potatoes and lingonberries.

19. Kottbullar: Kottbullar is a traditional Swedish dish of boiled beef and pork dumplings. It is usually served with mashed potatoes and lingonberries.

20. Rödbetssallad: Rödbetssallad is a popular Swedish salad made with beets, potatoes, and onions. It is usually served with hard-boiled eggs and mayonnaise.

ii. Dining Out in Sweden

Sweden is a great destination for food lovers looking to experience a unique culinary experience. Whether you are looking for traditional Swedish cuisine, international cuisine or a combination of both, Sweden has something for everyone.

For the traditional diner, there are a variety of restaurants that specialize in Swedish cuisine. These can be found throughout the country, in both cities and towns, and offer a wide range of dishes. Popular options include pickled herring, gravlax (marinated salmon), Swedish meatballs, and Janssons frestelse (a potato and anchovy casserole). For those looking for something more international, there are plenty of options as well. Italian, Chinese and Indian restaurants are easy to find, as are more exotic options such as Thai, Mexican and African.

When dining out in Sweden, it is important to remember that service charges are often included in the price of the meal, so don't be surprised if you don't need to leave a tip. It is also important to remember that many restaurants will not accept credit or debit cards, so make sure to bring enough cash for your meal.

The cost of dining out in Sweden can vary greatly depending on where you eat and what type of food you are looking for. In general, the cost of meals in the larger cities can be more expensive than those in smaller towns, but the quality of the food is usually very high.

Overall, Sweden is a great destination for food lovers looking to experience a unique culinary experience. With a wide range of options available, there is sure to be something to satisfy your cravings.

- *Dinning etiquette:*

Sweden is a modern and cosmopolitan country, so there is no strict set of rules when it comes to dining etiquette. However, there are some things that you should keep in mind when dining in Sweden.

First, it is polite to arrive on time to a dinner engagement. Swedes are almost always punctual and expect their guests to be as well.

Second, it is customary to take off your shoes when entering a home. If you are invited to someone's house for dinner, be sure to ask if it is okay to keep your shoes on.

Third, it is polite to wait to be seated. In Sweden, the host will decide where each guest should sit.

Fourth, it is customary to wait for the host or hostess to start eating before you begin. This rule also applies when visiting a restaurant.

Fifth, you should use your utensils properly. In Sweden, it is considered rude to place your utensils on the table. Instead, you should place them on the plate when you are done eating.

Sixth, it is polite to say thank you after the meal. It is customary to thank the host or hostess for the meal and express your appreciation for the meal.

Seventh, you should avoid talking with your mouth full. This is considered rude in Sweden and it is best to wait until you have finished eating before you start talking.

Lastly, it is polite to offer to help with the dishes after the meal. Even if the host or hostess does not accept your offer, it is still polite to offer.

By following these few tips, you can demonstrate that you have good manners when dining in Sweden.

iii. Local Drinks of Sweden

Sweden is home to many unique and delicious local drinks. Whether you're in the mood for a light beer, a sweet liqueur, or a strong spirit, there's something for everyone in Sweden's diverse beverage selection. Here are just a few of the local drinks that you should be on the lookout for during your visit to Sweden.

1. Glögg: Glögg is a traditional Swedish mulled wine made with red wine, spices, and sometimes with a little brandy or vodka added in. It is typically served during the holidays, or in the colder months. It is often enjoyed with

a few gingersnaps or almond biscuits on the side.

2. Snaps: Snaps is a traditional Swedish liquor made with potatoes, grains, and herbs like dill, anise, and caraway. It is commonly served as an aperitif, with a few snaps being drunk before a meal.

3. Kopparberg: Kopparberg is a Swedish beer that has been around since 1882. It is made with a mix of barley, hops, and yeast. It has a light, slightly sweet taste and can be enjoyed all year round.

4. Jakobsons: Jakobsons is a traditional Swedish beer made with a mix of barley, hops, and wheat. It is a dark beer that is often enjoyed with a meal, as it pairs well with Swedish dishes.

5. Alkoholfritt: Alkoholfritt is a non-alcoholic beer that is popular in Sweden. It has a light, crisp taste and is often enjoyed by those who do not want to consume alcohol.

6. Äppelcidervin: Äppelcidervin is a traditional Swedish cider made with apples. It has a sweet, tart taste and is often enjoyed as an aperitif or with a meal.

7. Drängöl: Drängöl is a traditional Swedish beer made with a mix of grains and hops. It is a dark beer that is slightly sweet and has a strong flavor.

8. Rököl: Rököl is a traditional Swedish beer made with smoked malt and hops. It is a dark beer that has a smoky flavor and is often enjoyed with a meal.

9. Gotlandsdricke: Gotlandsdricke is a traditional Swedish beer made with a mix of rye, wheat, and hops. It has a light, sweet taste and is often enjoyed with a meal.

10. Kvällsöl: Kvällsöl is a traditional Swedish beer made with a mix of barley, wheat, and hops. It is a dark beer that has a slightly sweet taste and is often enjoyed as an aperitif or with a meal.

11. Årgångsöl: Årgångsöl is a traditional Swedish beer made with a mix of grains and hops. It has a light, sweet taste and is often enjoyed with a meal.

12. Västerbottenost: Västerbottenost is a traditional Swedish cheese that is often enjoyed with a beer. It has a strong, salty flavor and is often enjoyed with a meal.

13. Punsch: Punsch is a traditional Swedish punch that is made with arrack, sugar, and spices. It is usually served cold and is often enjoyed as an aperitif or after-dinner drink.

14. Aquavit: Aquavit is a traditional Swedish spirit made with a mix of grains and spices. It is usually served cold and is often enjoyed as an aperitif or with a meal.

15. ölbröd: ölbröd is a traditional Swedish beer bread that is made with a mix of grains and hops. It is a dark bread that has a slightly sweet taste and is often enjoyed with a beer.

16. Vörtbröd: Vörtbröd is a traditional Swedish beer bread that is made with a mix of grains and hops. It is a light bread that has a slightly sweet taste and is often enjoyed with a beer.

17. Kalvöl: Kalvöl is a traditional Swedish beer made with a mix of grains and hops. It is a dark beer that has a slightly sweet taste and is often enjoyed as an aperitif or with a meal.

18. Mjöd: Mjöd is a traditional Swedish mead made with honey, spices, and grains. It has a sweet, slightly spicy taste and is often enjoyed as an aperitif or

with a meal.

19. Tuborg: Tuborg is a popular Swedish beer that has been around since 1873. It is made with a mix of grains and hops and has a light, slightly sweet taste.

20. Päroncider: Päroncider is a traditional Swedish cider made with pears. It has a sweet, fruity taste and is often enjoyed as an aperitif or with a meal.

Sweden is home to many unique and delicious local drinks. Whether you're looking for a light beer, a sweet liqueur, or a strong spirit, there's something for everyone. With its rich brewing and distilling tradition, Sweden is sure to have something to satisfy your taste buds.

ESSENTIAL INFORMATION

A. Visa and Documentation

When traveling to Sweden as a tourist, it is important to make sure that you have the correct visa and documentation to be able to enter the country. Depending on your nationality, you will likely need a visa to enter Sweden. All visitors from outside the European Union and the European Economic Area must apply for a visa in advance of their trip.

The first step in obtaining a visa for Sweden is to determine if you need one based on your nationality. If you do require a visa, you must apply for it at the Swedish embassy or consulate in your home country. You will need to provide the necessary documents, such as a valid passport, a copy of your flight itinerary, proof of sufficient funds, and other documents depending on your individual circumstances. Your application will be evaluated, and a visa will be provided if it is accepted.

If you are travelling to Sweden for a short stay (less than 90 days), you may be eligible for a Schengen visa. This visa allows you to visit other countries within the Schengen area, including Sweden, for up to 90 days in any 180-day period.

If you are traveling to Sweden for a longer stay (more than 90 days), you must apply for a residence permit. This permit is required for any stay over 90 days and must be applied for at least three months before your intended date of arrival in Sweden. You will need to provide the necessary documents, such as a valid passport, proof of sufficient funds, and other documents depending on your individual circumstances.

No matter what type of visa you are applying for, it is important to be aware of the entry and exit rules for Sweden. All visitors must carry a valid passport and visa with them at all times. It is also important to ensure that you have the necessary documentation for any activities you plan to do in Sweden, such as working, studying, or volunteering.

In addition to a visa and passport, all visitors should be aware of the current entry requirements for Sweden. As of 2021, all visitors must provide proof of a negative PCR test taken within 48 hours of their arrival in Sweden. It is also recommended that all travelers have comprehensive travel insurance to cover any unexpected costs or medical expenses while in Sweden.

Overall, it is important to make sure that you have the correct visa and documentation before traveling to Sweden. Be sure to check the Swedish embassy or consulate in your home country for the most up-to-date visa and entry requirements for Sweden.

B. Money and Currency

Sweden is a beautiful country with a rich culture, vibrant cities, and stunning landscapes. Before you visit, it's important to make sure you understand the country's currency and money system. Making the most of your stay will be easier if you do this.

In Sweden, the official currency is the Swedish krona (SEK). It is subdivided into 100 öre. Coins are available in denominations of 1, 2, 5, and 10 kronor, and notes in denominations of 20, 50, 100, 500, and 1000 kronor. Many of the coins have designs featuring animals (such as the moose and reindeer), as well as King Carl XVI Gustaf.

Most stores and restaurants in Sweden accept cash and cards. As of January 2021, Sweden is largely a cashless society, and the majority of Swedes prefer to pay with cards. Visa and Mastercard are the two most frequently used credit cards. American Express is also accepted in some places, but it's not as widely used.

When exchanging money in Sweden, it's always best to do so at a bank or currency exchange office. You can also use ATMs and some stores to exchange currency.

When it comes to tipping in Sweden, it's not mandatory, but it is appreciated. The general rule is to round up to the nearest krone. For example, if your bill is 133 SEK, you could leave a tip of 2 SEK.

It's important to remember that Sweden is a relatively expensive country to visit. Prices range from reasonably priced to quite high, depending on where you are and what you're doing. It's a good idea to check the prices of items before you buy them, to make sure you don't overspend.

By understanding Sweden's money and currency systems, you can make the most of your visit and have a great time in this beautiful country.

C. Health and Safety

Sweden is a great destination for travelers, offering a wide variety of activities, attractions, and experiences. However, it is important to stay safe and healthy while visiting Sweden. Here are some tips to help you stay safe and healthy while on your trip.

1. Be sure to check the weather before you travel. Sweden has some extreme weather conditions, so be sure to dress appropriately for the conditions. Wear layers and bring a waterproof jacket and/or raincoat.

2. Make sure you have a good travel insurance policy. Make sure it covers medical expenses, lost or stolen items, and any potential risks associated with your trip.

3. Be aware of your surroundings. Sweden has a low crime rate, but it is still important to be aware of your surroundings and take precautions to ensure your safety.

4. Be aware of the roads and traffic. In Sweden, it is illegal to drink and drive.

5. Be aware of the drinking age. In Sweden, the legal drinking age is 18.

6. Be aware of the laws and customs. Sweden has strict laws regarding drugs, alcohol, and violence. Be sure to obey the laws and respect the customs.

7. Be aware of the food safety regulations. Make sure to buy food from reputable sources and always wash your hands before eating.

8. Be aware of the medical facilities. If you need medical attention, make sure to find a reputable hospital or clinic.

9. Be aware of the water safety regulations. In Sweden, it is not advised to swim in natural bodies of water, as they may contain pollution or parasites.

10: Be aware of the wildlife. Wild animals should not be approached since they can be deadly.

By following these tips, you can ensure that your trip to Sweden is safe and enjoyable. Safe travels!

D. What to bring to Sweden

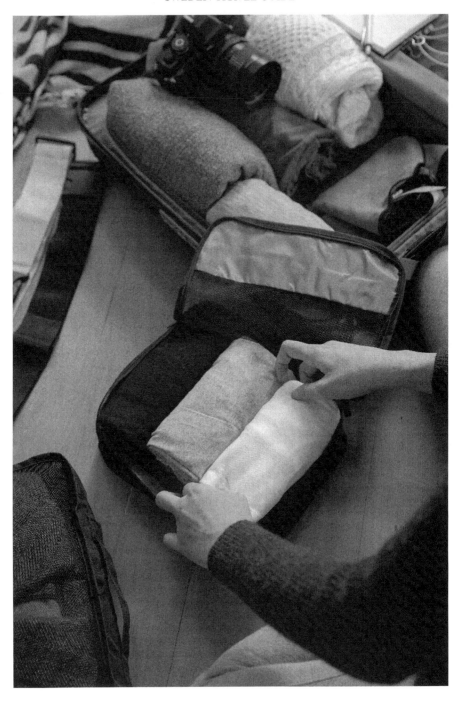

Here are some essential items to bring for a tourist visiting Sweden:

1. Clothing: Pack a variety of clothing for all types of weather. Sweden's climate can range from warm and sunny to cold and icy. Make sure to bring a rain jacket, a warm coat, a hat, gloves, and scarves to keep you warm and dry.

2. Shoes: Good-quality shoes are a must for any long walk. Bring comfortable shoes that can handle wet and slippery surfaces, as well as some boots if you plan to go hiking.

3. Electronics: Make sure to bring a reliable power adapter as well as a converter plug if you are bringing any electronics from abroad. A mobile phone is also essential for staying in touch with family and friends back home.

4. Currency: Sweden's currency is the Swedish krona (SEK). Make sure to bring enough cash for your trip, and exchange some of your dollars for krona before you arrive.

5. Maps and guidebooks: A good map or guidebook will help you find your way around the country. It's also a great way to get to know the culture and history of Sweden.

6. Camera: A camera is a must for recording all your memorable moments in Sweden. Make sure to bring extra memory cards, batteries, and a charger so you can capture all your experiences.

7 Rain gear: The weather in Sweden can be unpredictable, so you should pack a waterproof jacket and an umbrella.

8: Bring sunscreen and sunglasses. Make sure to bring sunscreen and sunglasses as the days can be quite sunny during the summer months.

9 Electricity adapter: Make sure to bring a European electricity adapter if

you plan on using any electronic devices while in Sweden.

Cash: While many places in Sweden accept credit and debit cards, it is still a good idea to bring some cash with you in case you need it.

11) Travel Insurance: Make sure to have travel insurance before coming to Sweden to protect yourself in case of any unforeseen events.

12 ID: Make sure to bring your passport or other form of identification with you in case you need to show it to local authorities.

These are some of the items you should bring with you when traveling to Sweden. Be sure to double check the list before leaving to make sure you don't forget anything important. Enjoy your trip!

CONCLUSION

S weden is an amazing country to visit and explore. With its stunning landscapes, fascinating culture, and delicious cuisine, it is no wonder that so many travelers choose it as their go-to destination. From the bustling cities of Stockholm and Gothenburg to the peaceful countryside, you can find something for everyone in Sweden. Whether you are looking for an adventurous outdoor holiday, a relaxing beach getaway, or a cultural experience, Sweden has it all. With its friendly locals, interesting history, and fantastic attractions, Sweden should be on everyone's list of places to explore.

Printed in Great Britain
by Amazon

21908489R00035